I feel BETTER NOW

How to feel okay on a difficult day

Dr. Wendy Down

illustrated by Dr. Charan Surdhar

THIS BOOK BELONGS TO:

First Printing: 2023
ALANNA RUSNAK PUBLISHING
ISBN: 978-1-990336-27-0

Alanna Rusnak Publishing is an imprint of Chicken House Press
282906 Normanby/Bentinck Townline
Durham, Ontario, Canada, N0G 1R0

Dear YOU

I wrote this book to help you know what to do any time you feel sad, angry, afraid, or overwhelmed.

After learning **Five Easy Steps**, you'll know exactly how to turn a feeling you don't like into a feeling you do like. Often in minutes!

If you are a parent, teacher, or someone who loves a child, this book is for you too.

As children learn the skills in this book, it can help for an adult to read alongside them.
You might even enjoy trying the
Five Easy Steps yourself!

We all have feelings. They are a natural part of us,
whether we are big or small, young or old.

There are many feelings we like, such as excitement or
happiness, cheerfulness or satisfaction, peace or pride.

There are other feelings we don't like, such as sadness or
fear, anger or embarrassment, worry or shame.

When we feel upset, we want to feel better. But how?

Our bodies have a superpower. They can help us turn feelings we don't like upside down! And it isn't hard to learn.

In this book, you'll learn to turn
worry into happiness,
upset into calm,
fear into bravery,
and nervousness into relaxation.

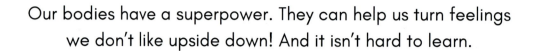

Changing feelings you *don't* like into feelings you *do* like is an amazing thing your body can do.

Many of us, including grown-ups, don't know how to feel better when we feel stressed or upset. But it is something that everyone can learn.

After you try it once, you will always know how to help yourself feel better on a difficult day.

Your body's superpower can work if you are at home, at school, on the playground, or at the doctor's office.

It can work if you are with other people or all by yourself.

It can work if you are being teased at school or are being left out.

It can work if you are watching a scary movie, having an argument, or are afraid of going to sleep.

No matter where you are and what you are doing, your body knows how to help you feel better when you are upset.

Would you like to start using this superpower your body has?

You will learn by taking **Five Easy Steps**. Before you learn them, here are a few facts to help you prepare:

Fact #1

Thinking about a feeling is not the same as feeling a feeling

THINKING

oh no... they're arguing again

they don't like me anymore...

When you think about a feeling, you are saying words in your mind. When you feel a feeling, you are feeling sensations in your body. Sensations are physical experiences like tightness, heaviness, or discomfort.

Your superpower works while you feel these sensations.

In this book, you will learn how to do this. And you will be surprised by what happens!

FEELING

I feel a knot in my stomach

there's a heavy feeling in my chest

Fact # 2

When you feel upset, it's a bit like feeling a bruise on the inside of your body.

Have you ever had a bruise? If so, you know that your body is uncomfortable where the bruise is. Outside the bruise, you feel fine.

The same thing is true of uncomfortable feelings. An upsetting feeling is a spot in your body that hurts on the inside. In this book, we will call these inside-bruises 'feeling spots.'

BRUISE

FEELING SPOT

Fact # 3

A feeling spot can be anywhere in your body.

It can be in your stomach, in your chest, in your throat,
or anywhere else.

Fact # 4

Your feelings spots are made of YOU.

They are safe to feel. They also love when you pay attention to
them and you never have to worry about doing it wrong!

Now that you know these facts, you are ready to learn the **Five Easy Steps** that let your superpower help a feeling spot.

1. Find your feeling spot.
2. Decide it's okay for your feeling spot to feel better.
3. Explore your feeling spot.
4. Play with your feeling spot.
5. Recheck your feeling spot.

Now that you know the **Five Easy Steps**, are you ready to try them on a feeling spot?

Easy Step #1

Finding your feeling spot

To find a feeling spot, think about a situation that you do not feel okay about right now. For example, what made you pick up this book? What makes you feel sad or anxious, mad or afraid?

As you think about this situation, imagine you are a detective looking for the feeling spot for that situation. Start by scanning your body.

You might like to close your eyes when you do this. Can you find a spot in your body that is uncomfortable right now? A spot that feels tight or tense, heavy or shaky? When you have found a spot inside your body that feels uncomfortable, you've completed **Easy Step #1**. You've found your feeling spot!

If you haven't found it yet, here are some things to try:

Pay attention to the middle of your body, where your tummy is. How does that area feel? Is it quiet and calm, or is it uncomfortable?

Move higher up in your body, where your chest is. How does it feel there?

As a feeling spot detective, you can feel everywhere inside your body, from your head to your toes, to find where your feeling spot is located. (And here's something tricky — sometimes, feeling spots can even be outside or around your body.)

It's possible you feel upset but can't find a feeling spot. What should you do then? Sometimes feeling spots can be spread out like smoke in the air or like a sound that lingers in your ears. If you can sense a feeling like that lingering in or around your body, you've found your feeling spot.

Now that you've found your feeling spot, your body will be able to use its superpowers to make it feel better!

11

Easy Step #2

Decide it's okay for your feeling spot to feel better

Now that you've found your feeling spot, you will make a choice about it. You are in charge of your body, and your body listens to you. When you are ready for your feeling spot to feel better, your superpowers will help this happen.

To do that, ask yourself: **"Is it okay with me if this feeling spot starts to feel better now?"**

If you decide it's okay for your feeling spot to feel better, you can let your body know this in whatever way you like.

You could nod your head to say, "Yes, it's okay."

You could tap your fingers gently over your feeling spot to say, "I'm ready for this spot to feel better now."

it's okay for my feeling spot to feel better...

Because you are being a detective, you could even make up a secret code — one that only you and your body would know. It's fun to have a secret way to talk with your body. You can't get this step (or any of the other steps) wrong, so try whatever you like!

12

Easy Step #3

Explore your feeling spot

Your next step is to be curious about your feeling spot.
Your body will use its superpower to help it feel better
and you'll want to notice what happens!

With your detective hat still on, pay close attention to your feeling spot
to understand what is happening as your superpower goes to work.

The only way to understand is — you guessed it! — to feel it closely.

**Your feeling spot will be very interesting to explore as it will
have details like shape, size, colour, and texture.**

To help you discover the details of your feeling spot,
use the questions on the following pages. Then you
can use your answers to draw a picture of yourself
and your feeling spot!

When you are ready to do this, grab your craryons or pencils and turn the page

Does your feeling spot have a size?

- watermelon
- grapefruit
- lemon
- tomato
- cherry

or... I'm not sure

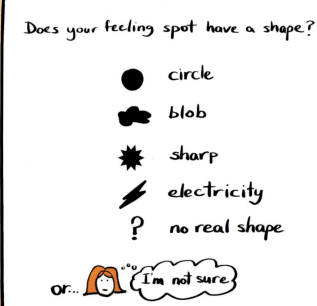

Does your feeling spot have a shape?

- circle
- blob
- sharp
- electricity
- no real shape

or... I'm not sure

Does your feeling spot have a color?

or... I'm not sure...

What is your feeling spot like?

- hard outside soft inside
- hard outside and inside
- rough outside and hard
- spongy
- squishy

or... I'm not sure

It's also fine if you don't know the answers to these questions or you can't tell right now. Remember, you can't get this wrong!

Does your feeling spot have a texture?

- hard
- spongy
- soft
- wavy
- bumpy
- cracked

or... I'm not sure

Does your feeling spot move?

- fast and swirly
- moving around
- crackling
- not moving
- bubbling

or... I'm not sure

What is the intensity of your feeling spot?

1

10

As a feeling spot detective, you might also be interested to notice how much bigger YOU are than your feeling spot.

To do that, notice the size of your feeling spot. Notice that all the upset is inside your feeling spot, like when you have a bruise. Outside the feeling spot, your body is comfortable and relaxed. Isn't that interesting?
Outside your feeling spot, your body already feels okay.

As you notice these details of your feeling spot, use the figures on the next two pages to draw it. If you like, you can also draw what your body feels like on the outside of the feeling spot. The outside may be very different from the inside and that will make your picture very interesting.

turn the page

As you answer some of the questions about your feeling spot, you might start to notice something happening.

Has your feeling spot started to change? Is it the same size as before or is it getting smaller? If it was hard before, is it getting softer now? Has it moved to a different place or spread out somehow? If its intensity was an eight before, what intensity number would you give it now?

If your feeling spot has started to change, your superpower has started to work. And you are learning a secret. Your mind talks in words but your body talks in sensations. As you pay attention to how your feeling spot feels, you feel better.

It makes sense! When you are sad or afraid or upset, do you feel better when someone listens to how you feel? Your feeling spots are the same! When you listen to what your body is saying by paying attention to your feeling spot, you feel better. It's actually kind of simple, isn't it?

If your feeling spot is starting to feel better as you pay close attention to it, are you ready to try something fun?

Easy Step #4

Play with your feeling spot

Feeling spots are made of your energy and some of them like to be played with. A soft one might like to be squished like clay, a hard one might like to be melted like ice, and a fluffy one might like to drift away like a cloud in the sky. Do you want to see if your feeling spot would like to play with you?

Playing with your feeling spot is actually very easy. You just use your imagination!

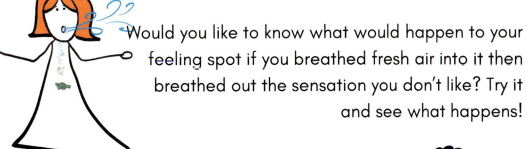

Would you like to know what would happen to your feeling spot if you breathed fresh air into it then breathed out the sensation you don't like? Try it and see what happens!

Would it be fun to picture your feeling spot like a piece of cheese that could be nibbled away by a hungry mouse? If it would, try it and see!

Maybe you can imagine your feeling spot being like a piece of ice slowly melting away in the sun.

You could also try tapping lightly on your feeling spot. See if that changes it in a way you like.

There is no wrong way to use your imagination to play with your feeling spot!

Picture something happening in your mind, then try it with your feeling spot. It will take a bit of time to tell, so be patient. Then feel your feeling spot again to find out what happened.

If you've been taking these **Easy Steps**, your feeling spot might have changed a lot. It might even have disappeared.

Have you ever sucked on a candy as it got smaller and smaller then finally dissolved? After the candy disappeared, you couldn't taste it anymore, could you?

Feeling spots are the same.

Once you've felt all the uncomfortable sensations in your feeling spot, none of it will be left anymore. You'll know your superpower is finished working when the place where your feeling spot used to be feels calm, peaceful, and okay. Like magic, your feeling spot will have disappeared and that area will feel relaxed and calm instead!

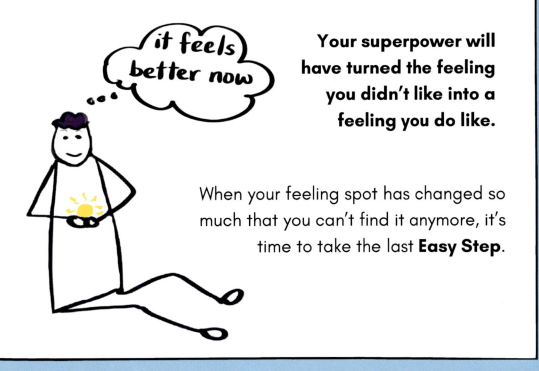

it feels better now

Your superpower will have turned the feeling you didn't like into a feeling you do like.

When your feeling spot has changed so much that you can't find it anymore, it's time to take the last **Easy Step**.

Easy Step #5

Recheck your feeling spot

Think again of the situation that made you open this book. Remember what was making you feel sad, mad, worried, or upset.

When you think of that situation again, recheck your feeling spot. How does it feel now?

If it was uncomfortable before, is it more comfortable now? If it felt tight like a knot before, does it now feel relaxed? If it was heavy before, is it light now?

Where your body didn't feel okay before, does it feel okay now?

If your body feels different now, congratulations! You've learned how to use your superpower.

If there is still a sensation you don't like in your feeling spot, that's okay too. Your superpower just needs a little more time to work with it.

When your feeling spot feels better, you can draw a picture of what it is like now.

You've now learned the **Five Easy Steps** to let your superpower turn a feeling you *don't* like into a feeling you *do* like. **What was it like to learn this?**

Were you surprised to think of feelings as spots?

Do you like knowing that your body has a superpower that can help you feel better any time you are upset?

Now that you know this, how will you use your superpower next?

One thing is for sure: the next time you feel worried, sad, angry, or upset, you can remember what you did with your feeling spot today. You'll know you can take the **Five Easy Steps** with your next feeling spot too.

Any time you need a reminder, this book is here to help you. Once you know the steps, you can also use your superpower without this book.

Every feeling spot is different and each one will respond to the **Five Easy Steps.** It can be fun to work with your feeling spots and, as you do, you will get better and better at using your superpower.

Feeling your feeling spots is very healthy for your body. You already know that lifting heavy weights helps your muscles become stronger, and in the same way, feeling your feeling spots help your superpower become stronger. That means, the more often you use it, the more easily you will be able to turn feelings you don't like into feelings you do like.

Remember: the feeling spots in your body are made of you. They are safe to feel and you can't do it wrong. And no matter how big or intense or uncomfortable a feeling spot is, YOU will always be bigger.

And you will know you can use the **Five Easy Steps** to help yourself feel okay even on a difficult day.

1. Find your feeling spot.

2. Decide it's okay for your feeling spot to feel better.

3. Explore your feeling spot.

4. Play with your feeling spot.

5. Recheck your feeling spot.

Reflection SPACE

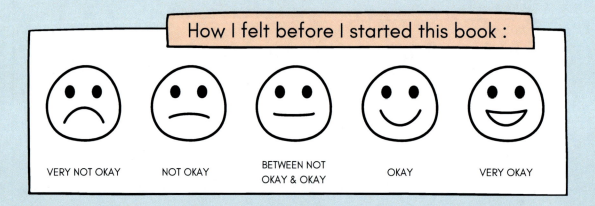

How I felt before I started this book :

| VERY NOT OKAY | NOT OKAY | BETWEEN NOT OKAY & OKAY | OKAY | VERY OKAY |

How I felt after finishing this book :

| VERY NOT OKAY | NOT OKAY | BETWEEN NOT OKAY & OKAY | OKAY | VERY OKAY |

Reflection SPACE

Do you have more to say about what you learned in this book? Use this page to write what you're thinking.

Reflection SPACE

Do you have more to draw about what you learned in this book? Use this page to draw what you're thinking.

A Closing Note FOR ADULTS

Thank you for helping a child learn the **Five Easy Steps** to feel okay even on a difficult day. These skills will help them navigate the challenges of life with skill, self-confidence, and stability. I can only imagine the difference it would have made in my own life to have learned these skills as a child. If you have ideas on how this book could reach more children (and adults) I'd love to hear from you. Contact me through *www.wendydown.com/book*.

Wendy Down is a Doctor of Integrative Medicine and a life coach who specializes in helping people learn the skills to achieve emotional well-being. She is based in Ontario, Canada. Find her online at *www.wendydown.com*.

Charan Surdhar is a Doctor of Integrative Medicine, geneticist, and part-time doodler who helps people change their stories to change their genetics. She is based in Birmingham, England. Find her online at *www.yourdnagift.com*.

Would you like to use this book in your classroom
or other group setting?

Visit *www.wendydown.com/book* where you can
download PDF copies of pages 16, 17, 23, and 28-30
to reproduce for your students.

Share your questions and stories
with the author there as well!

Made in the USA
Middletown, DE
28 February 2025

72022469R00021